CHURCHES & CATHEDRALS

MASTERPIECES OF ARCHITECTURE

Stacey McNutt

SMITHMARK

This edition published in 1996 by SMITHMARK Publishers,
a division of U.S. Media Holdings, Inc., 115 West 18th Street, New York, NY 10011.

SMITHMARK books are available for bulk purchase for sales promotion and premium use.
For details write or call the manager of special sales,
SMITHMARK Publishers, 115 West 18th Street, New York, NY 10011.

This book was designed and produced by Todtri Productions Limited
P.O. Box 572, New York, NY 10116-0572 FAX: (212) 279-1241

Printed and bound in Singapore

Library of Congress Catalog Card Number 97-066040
ISBN 0-7651-9221-7

Author: Stacey McNutt

Publisher: Robert M. Tod
Editorial Director: Elizabeth Loonan
Book Designer: Mark Weinberg
Senior Editor: Cynthia Sternau
Project Editor: Ann Kirby
Photo Editor: Edward Douglas
Picture Researchers: Meiers Tambeau, Laura Wyss
Production Coordinator: Jay Weiser
Desktop Associate: Paul Kachur
Typesetting: Command-O Design

CONTENTS

INTRODUCTION

The story of church architecture is one of faith, ambition, and innovation—innovations which enabled architects to plan and build churches and cathedrals of unsurpassed beauty.

From the fourth century to the present day, church builders have followed in the tradition of the first Christians who built shrines in the holy places where Jesus and His apostles lived, taught, and performed miracles. They have attempted to construct buildings which magnify Christ's earthly life and enshrine the fullness of its promise.

The earliest Christian churches were humble structures of wood or clay, or brick and concrete. Some were no more than an altar where a few could gather to feel Christ's mysterious presence and remember the lessons of His teachings. Such gatherings were initially discouraged by the Romans. In A.D. 135, the emperor Hadrian attempted to eliminate the new religion in the Holy Land. At the site of Christ's nativity, where Christians frequently came to pray, Hadrian built a shrine to Adonis, and planted a sacred grove to the pagan gods.

The majority of the early Christians met in private rooms and caves. In times of persecution, they met in underground catacombs. The well-preserved frescoes in Rome's catacombs of St. Callixtus show what the decoration of the early churches must have been like. The subjects of the gallery frescos are many. Among them are the stories of the Good Shepherd and Jonah and the Fish. Loaves and wine represent the Eucharist; broken pots and birds in flight describe the release of the spirit after death, and serve as reminders of Christ's promise of everlasting life.

In A.D. 313, the Roman emperor Constantine the Great gambled shrewdly on the future of Christianity and issued an edict that made Christianity the state religion. Under Constantine's administration, with the supervision of his mother, Helena, imperial ministers began identifying the holy places where Christ had preached, reflected, and been laid to rest.

RIGHT: The eleventh-century Romanesque chapel of St. Michél is poised on a high, narrow pinnacle of solidified lava (puys), accessible only by a steep flight of stairs. The chapel's dramatically isolated location is reminiscent of nearly-inaccessible, cliffside monasteries in Greece. *Le Puy City, France.*

In A.D. 330, Constantine laid the cornerstone for the new Christian capital of the Roman Empire, Constantinople, and inaugurated the first great period of church-building. On Constantine's orders, more than two hundred churches were constructed in Palestine. The first churches covered the sites significant to the life of Christ and his followers. (Hadrian had conveniently marked the site of the nativity.) These churches were built in the form of Roman basilicas and martyria. Enough of these early churches survive to give us an impression of what they must have been like.

The Early Churches

The basilica, a rectangular hall with a wooden roof, was the traditional form of Roman civic buildings. The central space of the church was flanked by twin arcades or colonnades separating the central space from the side aisles. The arcade was surmounted by a wall with clerestory windows. The altar was in a semicircular or apsed space at the end of the colonnade. Pavements of marble or tiled mosaics drew the worshiper forward from one end of the church to the other and created a "sacred way," much like the Greek and Roman colonnaded roads that led to ancient temples and sanctuaries.

The exteriors of these churches tended to be plain. It was the interior, especially the apse, that sheltered the altar and received the most decoration. The apse was often adorned with jewel-like mosaics—an art form that scholars believe was perfectly suited to the early church because of its formal and hieratic composition.

Few of the original churches built in the Holy Land still survive. One of these is the Church of the Nativity in Bethlehem, built above the grotto where Christ was born. The original mosaics beneath the wooden floor of the nave suggest the former interior beauty of the church. The original building was reconstructed in A.D. 530 by the emperor Justinian after its destruction by the Samaritans. It has had many variations in fortune since, but it is still much like the church which Constantine built.

The finest existing examples of the early basilicas are in Rome. The Santa Maria Maggiore is a large church, comparable to Old St. Peter's. Its long nave is flanked by Ionic columns under a flat entablature. The elaborate mosaic panels above the columns date back to the fifth century, and tell stories from the Old Testament. Both the Santa Sabina—built in the fifth century—and the St. Paolo Fuori have been meticulously restored, and are excellent examples of churches in the Constantinian style.

The second type of church structure, the martyrium, consisted of a circular or octagonal space. The first Church of the Holy Sepulchre, built over the rock tomb where Christ was laid, was built in the circular, domed style of the Roman martyrium. The main church was a large rotunda supported by concentric pillars which formed an ambulatory for pilgrims to walk around the tomb. It also had clerestory windows in the walls above the pillars.

The Church of the Holy Sepulchre has been rebuilt, altered, and repaired many times since its construction. Today, pilgrims can see the two rock sides that remain of the Sepulchre in the restored church rebuilt by the Byzantine emperor Constantine Monomachos in 1048, and restored by the Crusaders in 1149.

The Divide Between East and West

During the time of Christ, the Roman Empire was vast, encompassing Northern Africa, Arabia, and the countries around the Mediterranean. It extended as far east as Armenia and as far west as Great Britain. Its administration was Roman, but its culture and philosophy were Greek.

The empire was not an entirely unified one, and differences, especially in the form of worship in Christian churches, soon emerged. These differences would shape the form of church architecture. In Rome, the Church practiced a congregational form of worship. It preferred the basilica with its long approach. The additions of transepts created a church in the shape known as the Latin cross, physically orientated from the East to the West, in the mystical equation of Christ with the rising sun.

LEFT: Italian Gothic and Romanesque architecture was influenced by the classical buildings of the Roman Empire. The interior columns and arcades of Tuscan cathedrals were ornamented with marbled cladding and patterned floors, much like the ancient basilicas. The interior of the Cathedral at Pisa is one of the most beautiful in the Tuscan style. *Pisa, Italy.*

FOLLOWING PAGE: The imperial viceroys of the Roman Empire ruled from Ravenna. The city's early Byzantine churches equalled the beauty of those in Constantinople, and are among the best preserved. The grotto-like interior of S. Vitale is covered with scenes from the Old Testament. In this lunette, Abraham entertains the angels. *Ravenna, Italy.*

The eastern Church, however, was inclined toward the more mystical properties of the circle, preferring the centralized form of the martyrium for worship. It also held very strict views about the hierarchical representation of Christ, who was always centrally placed at the top of the church.

The eastern Church adopted the radial, or cross-in-square, plan of the Greek cross. A central space was usually covered by a principal dome. Arms or extensions were covered by subsidiary domes. One arm was provided with an apse for the altar, now removed from the center of the building, and another with a narthex or porch. Decoration took the form of a continuous sheathing of marble and mosaic.

Compared to the long naves of the basilica, the circular enclosure of the martyrium was intimate. The dome was used in eastern churches to perfectly represent heaven; its most perfect example is the Hagia Sophia of Constantine's old city, now modern-day Istanbul.

The Hagia Sophia represents the early maturity of the Byzantine style of church architecture. Completed in A.D. 537 by the

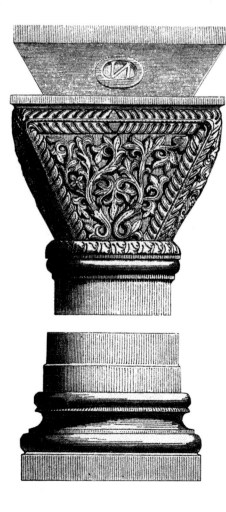

RIGHT: The capitals of columns were one of the few sculpted decorations in the Byzantine church, and the Byzantine decorative technique of twining leaves and vines became common in Romanesque churches throughout Western Europe.

emperor Justinian, it was the crown in the architectural jewel that was Constantinople, and its beauty and structural perfection was so complete that it became the model for churches throughout the eastern empire.

The empire that Justinian inherited in the early sixth century was a fractured one. Rome had fallen to the Ostrogoths in A.D. 476. The Vandals had established themselves in North Africa, and had invaded Spain. The Visigoths were in southern France, and the Franks were in the north. Bertrand Russell describes the fifth century as "a century of destructive action, which, however, largely determined the lines upon which Europe was to be developed."

Justinian attempted to retake as much of the western empire as he could. In A.D. 535, he invaded Italy and waged war against the Goths, recapturing Rome. He also warred against the Vandals in North Africa. However, neither territory remained fully within his grasp, and after his death in A.D. 565 the Lombards invaded Italy, and the western empire fell. The Dark Ages began.

During this time, centralized authority was preserved only in the Church. When the western empire fell, the Church, which had been the teacher of religion to a highly civilized society, became the sole civilizing force in western and central Europe. Monastic communities became the preserves of literary, scientific, technical, and artistic skills—islands of civilization.

The Church's reaction to this political turbulence was a strong movement to found monasteries and Christianize the people of Europe. Monastic life, which had been almost completely devoted to a life of seclusion and contemplation, became more active. The Benedictines devised a way of life that was equally divided between spiritual devotion and the survival of Christianity. They became the dominant order.

Many expected the world to end in the years 1000 and 1033. When these dates passed without event, a new period of church-building began. Monasteries began building churches commensurate with the Church's power and importance. Architecture was not one of the cloister arts, so the new churches were forged by trial and error. The new style was called Romanesque. Its mature form is a massive one, and combines Roman, Byzantine, Celtic, Saracenic, Carolingian, and Ottonian elements of structure and design.

The unifying elements in this stylistic mix were the interest of the Roman Catholic Church and the needs of the great monasteries and abbeys for larger places of worship to accommodate growing communities and an influx of pilgrims, whose donations were often the sole source of the abbey's income.

LEFT: Rouen is known as the City of a Hundred Spires, none of them taller than the Cathedral of Notre-Dame. Its iron spire, known as the Butter Tower, was completed in the seventeenth century. *Rouen, France.*

But the architects of early Romanesque churches were engaged in an unceasing experiment in the face of calamitous fires and faulty building techniques. The necessity for replacing dangerous wooden roofs with those of vaulted stone resulted in a new architectural style.

The Gothic Cathedral

A new era of church-building began in France in 1130. Henri Sangler's design for the Cathedral of Sens reduced the size of the transept and produced a three-story nave that employed ribbed vaulting. The reconstruction of the Benedictine church of St.-Denis near Paris in 1140 took this design a step further: The ambulatory had vaults supported by slender columns, reducing the massive supporting walls of the Romanesque church and allowing more light to penetrate the interior. Thus the Gothic cathedral was born.

The Gothic style became the most common type of church architecture in most of Europe (except Italy) by the thirteenth century. Its rise signaled the cultural rebirth of Europe and the end of feudalism. The Gothic cathedral was not just a monument to man's spiritual aspirations, it also enhanced or established a city's prestige and importance. The largest

building in every medieval town was the church, whose Gothic gable and spires rose majestically over the rooftops of all the other buildings.

Building these massive churches was a lengthy and expensive undertaking. Churchmen and civic leaders often turned to bankers to finance the building of a city cathedral or the rebuilding of a damaged church. But the extraordinary amount of time required to complete a cathedral was often due to delays in financing, when original agreements fell apart.

The structural form of the cathedral developed out of the effort to build simple and beautiful churches completely vaulted in stone. This new form solved many of the problems of Romanesque church architecture while incorporating many of its basic features—nave, transept, choir, crypt, side aisles, and clerestory windows—without the mass of the Romanesque cathedral's walls and round arches.

The Renaissance and Baroque Styles

The modern—as opposed to the medieval—outlook began with revival of classical learning in Italy in the fifteenth century. This revival was paralleled by an equal passion for the austere beauty of classical design. The Renaissance was a time of intellectual inquiry stimulated by the fresh idea of man's temporal importance. Humanism was a philosophy that magnified man's

ABOVE: Gothic sculpture was altogether more naturalistic than Romanesque, as can be seen by the majestic, free-standing sculptures in front of the Rose Window on the west façade of Notre-Dame. Directly below is the King's Gallery with twenty-eight kings of Judah. *Notre-Dame, Paris, France.*

importance and intensified the importance of the individual; regional and national styles gave way to individual expression in art and architecture.

Renaissance architecture attempted to adapt the classical form of Roman temples to the design of Christian churches, and the dome began to replace the spire. Geometry gained new importance, and the circle employed in architecture became the symbol of God's perfection.

But the spirit of inquiry engendered by the Renaissance turned into the spirit of revolt in the northern regions, where the dominance of the Roman Catholic Church was resented. The revolt became the Reformation when Martin Luther, fueled by fury at the sale of indulgences, began to preach the doctrine of salvation by faith alone, rather than by works. On October 31, 1517, Luther drew up a list of ninety-five theses on indulgences that denied the right of the Pope to forgive sins, and nailed them to the church door at Wittenberg.

The effect of the Reformation on church architecture was the destruction of the relative unity of purpose it had previously enjoyed. Protestants wanted preaching auditoriums. They were opposed to the worship of images and the representation of the supernatural; some were offended by resplendent images in pilgrimage churches.

The Catholic Church responded by emphasizing the aspects of faith that most offended the Protestants, such as the intercession of saints and the holiness of relics. The development of the extravagant Baroque style coincided with the Counter-Reformation and was suitable for exploitation by the Catholic Church against Protestantism.

The Baroque style prevailed throughout the seventeenth and eighteenth centuries, partly because of the zeal with which the Jesuits administered the goals of the Counter-Reformation. But Church history does not stop here.

The religious movements of the nineteenth century reacted to the new influence of science, and architects and churchmen looked back on the beauty of old forms for inspiration. During this time, old forms of church architecture were influenced by new inventions; among these—and the main innovation—was the experimental use of iron as a structural element.

A new and enduring form of church architecture evolved from the designs and influence of Sir Christopher Wren (1632–1723), whose buildings exhibit a remarkable elegant, order, and dignity. The new simplicity was perfectly suited to the American colonies and the construction of places of worship in the New World.

BELOW: Brunelleschi's octagonal dome of Florence's Cathedral was completed between 1420 and 1434. The ribbed design is Gothic, but the decorative elements are purely classical, influenced by the architect's study of classical buildings in Rome. *Florence, Italy.*

CHAPTER ONE

BYZANTINE AND ROMANESQUE ARCHITECTURE

ABOVE: This illustration of the Hagia Sophia shows how architects built a dome over a square space. The innovative descending construction of domes and semi-domes transferred the weight of the vast central dome outward.

In A.D. 330, the Byzantine Empire was founded when the first Christian Roman emperor, Constantine the Great, moved the center of government east from Rome to its new, impregnable location on the Bosphorus—Byzantium. Constantine claimed that the location of the city we know as Constantinople or Istanbul appeared to him in a dream.

From the very beginning, Constantinople was meant to be a city of divine magnificence. Craftsmen, artists, and builders from all over the Mediterranean were commissioned to create a city that would embody the new Christian order in which church and state were one. Constantine's successors, Theodosium and Justinian, continued the work of making Constantinople a city of unrivaled splendor. When Constantine's original basilica-style Church of the Holy Wisdom was destroyed by riots in A.D. 532, Justinian saw his opportunity to rebuild an even more splendid church.

He commissioned two engineers, Isidore of Miletus and Anthemius of Tralles, to create a church that would be the religious focus of the empire. They accomplished their task within the remarkably short period of five years. When the emperor Justinian stepped inside the Hagia Sophia—the Church of the Holy Wisdom—and walked underneath its shimmering skin of mosaics, and stood underneath the dome that appeared to hang unsupported from heaven, he exulted: "I have surpassed Solomon!"

RIGHT: The Hagia Sophia as it looks today. The buttresses were added to reinforce the walls from earthquake damage, and to provide additional support for the vast dome. The Turks erected the minarets after they conquered Constantinople. *Istanbul, Turkey.*

LEFT: Dmitri's Chapel was built in 1193, two hundred years after the conversion of Grand Duke Vladimir to Orthodox Christianity. The exterior is decorated with sculpted reliefs that "sing" the Psalms of David. *Vladimir, Russia.*

BELOW: Between 1204 and 1461, Trabzon was the capital of an independent Greek empire, and one of the main intellectual centers of Hellenism and Christian Orthodoxy. The church of St. Sophia was built in 1204 and is Trabzon's best preserved building. St. Sophia's thirteenth-century frescoes are considered the finest in Byzantine art. *Trabzon, Turkey.*

No one contradicted Justinian, and no one would argue with him today, even though the interior of the Hagia Sophia is marred from its subsequent years of service as a mosque. The church, a religious museum since 1935, is one of the architectural wonders of the ancient world. Its vast, impressive dome is supported by pendentives which enabled the architects to support a circle on a square base. Isidore of Miletus and Anthemius of Tralles were the first architects to use pendentives to support a dome, and this invention's architectural importance has been compared to that of the arch and the vault.

The Hagia Sophia

The pendentives supporting the Hagia Sophia's large, crowning dome are inverted, concave triangles that spring from the four corners of the ground plan. They are stabilized by colossal arching piers connected by round arches 100 feet (30.5 meters) across. The eastern and western ends of the structure are extended by semicircular spaces. Each of these spaces is covered by a half-dome of the same diameter as the central dome, and each half-dome rests upon three small semi-domes. This creates a descending system of thrust and counter-thrust within the structure.

The side aisles are constructed in two stories (the upper gallery was exclusively for women); decorated marble arcades separate these aisles from the nave. The entrance at the west end of the building is a long, narrow narthex with doors that open to the nave and the side aisles.

This construction allowed the architects to build a huge space without breaking up the area with columns. It also changed the axis of the church, which as a basilica had been horizontal. Now, the eye is drawn upward, where light pours in through the windows in the upper and lower domes. The vaulted interior, ornamented with brilliantly colored mosaics, rises curve upon curve.

The frescos and mosaics on the semicircular walls lead the eye up to the central image of Christ, represented within the crown of the central dome. The saints and fathers of the early Church on the lower walls point up to the Old Testament prophets and evangelists, who appear detached from the world. They, in turn, move toward the base of the dome, where the Apostles and angels point upward to the Virgin and the image of God incarnate.

The effect is one of weightless space and light, a surprising openness in which the central dome appears to hang unsupported from heaven. It is as though the mysteries of heaven are revealed and brought down to earth. The achievements of the Hagia Sophia established the form and function of the Byzantine church, as well as the hierarchy of the representation of God in Heaven.

Church builders throughout the eastern empire converted basilicas into the domed cruciform churches. The liturgy of the eastern Church has remained largely unchanged. There was no need for a chancel or choir. The only change to the interior of the church was the addition of an iconostasis—a screen decorated with icons that stretches from one wall to the other, and separates the congregation from the sanctuary. The clergy perform most of the service at the altar behind this screen, emerging into the nave only briefly through the doors in the iconostasis.

No other church builders tried to match or surpass the size of the Hagia Sophia's central dome, which measures 107 feet (33 meters) in diameter and 180 feet (55 meters) high. The cascading domes of Greek churches are smaller and more slender, but the mosaics and frescos completed in the tenth, eleventh, and twelfth centuries, especially those at Daphni, Osios Loukas, and in the church of the Saviour in Chora, are unparalleled in their devotional beauty and expression. The scale and proportion of these Greek churches was copied throughout the Balkans for almost a thousand years.

RIGHT: In this late Byzantine mosaic of Christ the Judge at the Hagia Sophia, Christ's solemn expression is given a gentleness by the thirteenth-century artist's delicate technique and use of color. The mosaic's luminescence conveys a portion of the Hagia Sophia's former radiance. *Istanbul, Turkey.*

RIGHT: The distinctive three-barred cross of the Russian Orthodox Church crowns each of the extravagantly patterned domes and spires of St. Basil's Cathedral in Moscow. Built in the 1550s by Ivan IV, the Cathedral combines nearly every element of the late Byzantine style. It is now a historical museum. *Moscow, Russia.*

RIGHT: The fantastic cluster of the twenty-two domes give the Russian Cathedral of Transfiguration on Kizhi Island the appearance of a holy fortress. Constructed in 1744 without any nails, the shingled domes and church are made entirely of aspen.

The Eastern Empire

Services in the Byzantine Church were performed in the region's local dialect or language. Christianity was accepted in Kiev in the tenth century and Byzantine influence grew increasingly stronger thereafter. The Byzantine Church's Christianization and conquest of the Slavs and Bulgars brought literacy as well as Christian faith to the Slavonic countries. Two monks from Thessalonica, Cyril and Methodius, invented the Slavonic alphabet and made possible the translation of the Bible and Greek liturgy. This mission spread the Byzantine church style north, and established national churches in Christianized areas.

Russia embraced the Christianity of the eastern Church when it emerged as a nation in the thirteenth century. The Byzantine style was adopted in its pure form, before domes were modified to accommodate the weight of heavy snowfalls. Wood was used for church construction throughout western Russian—including frontier areas such as Kodiak, Alaska. Those of wooden churches became fantastically elaborated and decorated. St. Basil's in Moscow is a fanciful assemblage of onion domes and spires. Interiors of eastern churches were often dim, creating a sense of confinement as well as the mysterious atmosphere of an exalted chamber.

BELOW: Russian and Slavic churches were often decorated with illustrations of the twelve great festivals. The last, the Last Judgement, announces Christ's resurrection, vividly depicted in this sixteenth-century mural. Satan holds Judas in his lap, and rides an all-devouring two-headed serpent through a sea of sinners. *Morača, Yugoslavia.*

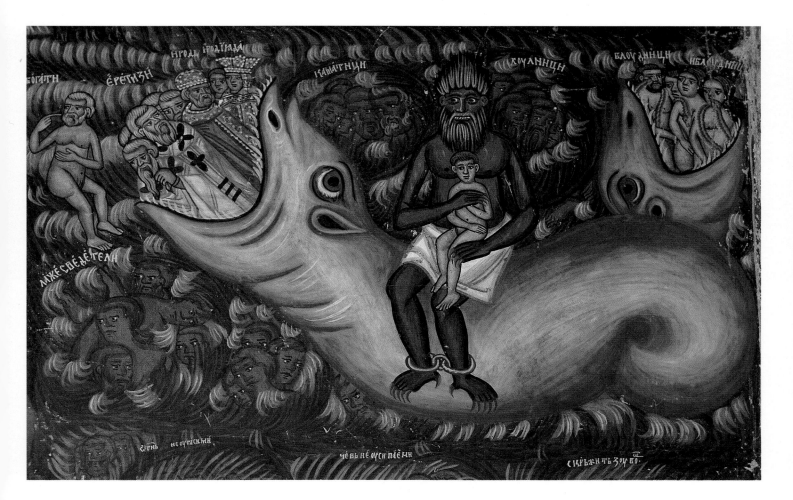

LEFT: Through its mission to the Russians and Slavs, the Greek Orthodox church survived the fall of the Byzantine Empire. The ascendent Serbian Empire built new churches and monasteries throughout Serbia and on Mount Athos. This painting shows the construction of the monastery at Morača. *Morača, Yugoslavia.*

ABOVE: Peč became the holy city of the Orthodox Serbs in the thirteenth century, when Archbishop Arsenus I transferred the patriarchate and established three churches on a mountainside outside the city: St. Demetrius, the Church of the Virgin, and the Church of the Holy Apostles, adorned with magnificent frescoes. *Peč, Yugoslavia.*

RIGHT: The Church of the Resurrection is one of imperial splendor. It was built in the late nineteenth century on the Griboedova Canal in St. Petersburg, on the site where Tsar Alexander II, "the Liberator," was assassinated by a bomb in 1881.

ABOVE: The conversion of the Slavs and Russians expanded the realm of Byzantine painting, and made possible the reconstruction of its history. Here, surrounded in a cloud of iridescent blue, an all-seeing Christ looks down to earth. The central medallion appears to be supported by saints and archangels. Prophets on the four "corners" hold parchment texts in their hands. *Morača, Yugoslavia.*

LEFT: Angels and apostles witness Christ's tender embrace of his mother's soul—beautifully symbolized in the form of a winged infant. Careful restoration has returned the frescoes (originally completed in 1295) to their original condition. *Dormition of the Virgin, St. Clements, Ochrid, Macedonia.*

BELOW: The blue domes and central gold dome of the Cathedral of the Assumption were completed in 1585. They shine in the sun beside the baroque belltower and St. Sergius Church in the monastic complex at Zagorsk. From here St. Sergius directed his mission to convert Russia and expand Russian monasticism. *Zagorsk, Russia.*

ABOVE: The vast interior of St. Mark's Basilica, like the interior of an early, great Byzantine church, shimmers with a radiant "skin" of marble and mosaics. This richness of decoration has given it the name *Chiesa d'Oro. Venice, Italy.*

Byzantine Architecture in the West

The development of the Byzantine style in the West can be seen on Italy's Adriatic coast in the city of Ravenna, famous for its well-preserved Byzantine mosaics. The church of San Vitale, built by Justinian's architects in A.D. 547, is composed of two concentric octagons forming a central space bounded by an aisle with vaults and galleries. The dome is made from clay pots fitted into each other, then covered with a tiled timber roof. The ingeniously light construction of the dome required no buttressing and is supported solely by arches.

St. Mark's basilica in Venice is an ornate example of the late Byzantine style in church architecture. Modeled on the Church of the Apostles in Constantinople and built in the eleventh century, St. Mark's is based on a Greek cross plan. Its gilded timber domes mark the center and arms of the cross. Its mosaics, created during the twelfth through the fourteenth centuries—among the finest in the world—were very probably executed by artists from Constantinople.

Venice shamelessly participated in the plunder of Constantinople with the Franks during the Fourth Crusade in 1204. The main altar, under which the evangelist rests, is encrusted with sacred enamels looted from the heart of Byzantium. The four bronze horses above the west portal, now in the Museum of San Marco, were also stolen during that time.

The End of an Empire

In 1453, a thousand years after the reign of Justinian, the Ottomans took Constantinople. They converted the Hagia Sophia into a mosque, and its interior decoration was white-washed. (Since 1935, when the Hagia Sophia was made a religious museum by the Turkish government, many of its mosaics have been uncovered.)

The Ottomans boasted that they had captured the heart of Christendom. But in truth, the heart of Christendom had been divided since the fall of Rome. A new, massive architectural style had already developed in the West. It demonstrated the growing strength and power of the western Church, and identified itself with the builders of ancient Rome.

The Romanesque Style

While Justinian's architects were building the church that was the consummate expression of heaven on earth, western Europe was being transformed by Germanic and Norse invaders. By the end of the sixth century, all former Roman provinces had become independent kingdoms.

In the tenth century, there was enough political stability to allow the clergy to build cathedrals that matched their power, authority, and wealth. Romanesque architecture emerged around the year 1000 and lasted until 1150. The monumental Romanesque style was forged, by trial and error, in the great abbey churches of western Europe.

The earliest stone churches preserved the rectangular design of the Roman basilica. The builders re-used bricks, concrete, and columns from Roman temples and buildings. The stone churches of the Saxons in Great Britain include remnants from

LEFT: This illustration shows the use of the round or Roman arch that gave the name Romanesque to medieval churches of vaulted stone. Shown this way, the arches of triforium and clerestory can be seen as a decorative motif. *Church of the Holy Trinity, Normandy, France.*

the buildings of their Roman predecessors. The beamed ceilings were made completely of wood.

Because their ceilings were constructed of wood, pilgrim churches—often the sites of torch-lit processions—were frequently destroyed in disastrous fires. These churches were built in an elongated cruciform shape to accommodate these very processions. When the flat, wooden roof was replaced by stone vaultings, the portico of the basilica was transformed into elongated transepts for purposes of abutment.

This new construction changed the old rectangle of the basilica into the church nave. A choir, a feature not found in eastern churches, was installed beyond the chancel arch. The sanctuary moved beyond the choir to the apse end. In the larger churches, the sanctuary was surrounded by an ambulatory.

The problem of counteracting the thrust, or outward pressure, of high, heavy nave vaults without obscuring clerestory windows was a determining factor in Romanesque design.

LEFT: The portals and the blind arches on the upper gallery of St. Mark's façade are decorated with seventeenth- and eighteenth-century mosaics. The mosaic shown here is on the upper gallery. *Venice, Italy.*

ABOVE: St. Mark's is constructed on the general plan of the Holy Apostles Church in Constantinople. Completed in 1073, the church has been continuously modified to accommodate the precious objects Venetian traders were charged by law to render on their return to "The House of St. Mark." *Procession in St. Mark's Square* by Gentile Bellini, 1496.

RIGHT: The tympanum, the semi-circular space above the doorway of the medieval church, was often decorated with sculpture. Christ in Glory or in Judgement was a favorite subject. Shown here is the decoration around the doorway to the Church of Semur, Brionnais.

The barrel vaults imperfectly balanced the extremely heavy walls characteristic of Romanesque architecture. To cope with the heavy centering required during the construction of these great vaults, ceilings were divided into independent, ribbed sections. The ponderous majesty of the Romanesque church is the result of the means required to support the stone ceilings. The sheer size of the columns in the nave of churches such as Durham still impresses modern visitors.

Other features which are considered characteristically Romanesque—raised sanctuaries, extensive crypts, ambulatories, and upper galleries—were all built to house relics and to accommodate the pilgrims who came to see them.

The Church of St. Foy, built between 1050 and 1130 in the valley of Conques in southern France, was one of the great abbey churches. The plan of St. Foy was designed with a system of continuous aisles that extended into the transept and allowed pilgrims to circulate through the sanctuary. The apse at the east end of the church opens outward into a number of encircling small chapels.

This type of construction is called a *chevet*, and it became part of the regular plan of French churches. Galleries around the upper nave and choir were constructed to allow devotees to circle above the sanctuary. Called a triforium, this design created an "upper room."

Benedictine abbeys in England built some of the largest and longest churches, including Winchester, Ely, and Norwich cathedrals. The Benedictines reserved the eastern end of the church entirely for the monks. The naves were reserved for the laity, and grew to impressive lengths.

Central towers became integral to massive Romanesque design and grew to impressive size. Twin towers, usually square, were a feature of the west end of churches in Normandy and England. At Speyer Cathedral, begun in 1030 by Conrad III, the four towers of enormous scale create a vast structure, symbolic of the power and authority of the German emperors who commissioned it.

Romanesque churches such as Speyer evidence the clergy's allegiance to the feudal states that ruled western and central Europe. The stern portrayal of Christ the Judge or Christ in Majesty in the center of the semicircular tympana over the entrance doors of Romanesque churches likens Him to an all-seeing feudal overlord, surrounded by apostles and angels.

LEFT: Towers became a feature of the Romanesque church, and were often added to make the building more majestic. Square twin towers were a feature of the west end of churches in Normandy and in England. *Cathedral St-Pierre, Lisieux, Normandy.*

Decorative Genius

The art of monumental sculpture was revived in western Europe during the Romanesque period after almost six hundred years of dormancy. Relief sculpture on the capitals of columns and around the massive doors of churches was used to depict biblical history and Church doctrine. Sculpted decoration began to cover many surfaces not previously embellished. Portals and the edges of arcade arches were especially rich in symmetrically carved devices including chevrons, dog-tooth, and pyramid patterns; angels, fantastic beasts, and human heads were also used. Some of the most fanciful and bizarre of these decorations can be seen in the imaginary animals on the capitals in the crypt of Canterbury Cathedral.

Shafts of the side columns were often sculpted with human forms. Among the most fantastic are the elongated human figures on the side columns at Moissac in southern France. Hybrid beasts climb over each other next to prophets holding scrolls that foretell the birth of Christ. The grotesqueness of the animal and human forms is a consequence of the Romanesque artist's disinclination to represent humans and animals in realistic dimensions. This enhanced the seemingly mystical inspiration of the figures.

Blind arcading was another decorative achievement of the Romanesque style. Blind arcades—which extended along

ABOVE: Constructed in the eleventh century in the red brick for which Toulouse is known, St-Sernin in Toulouse was among the grandest of the "pilgrimage churches." The design of the ambulatories has been incorporated in the arcades of the cathedral's distinctive tower. *St-Sernin Cathedral, Toulouse, France.*

ABOVE: Shown here are the chevron and crossing patterns on columns from Norman churches and decorated capitals, including twining foliage and a fantastic beast, like those in the *Book of Kells*. The portion of the arch shown here can be found in the Chapel of Galilee at Durham Cathedral.

ABOVE: The portion of Cormac's Chapel shown here illustrates a barrel vault and blind arcading. The chapel was consecrated in 1143, and is a remarkable example of the penetration of Romanesque architecture and decoration to an isolated center of Christian life. *Cashel Rock, Ireland.*

walls—sometimes were stacked in rows above one another, separated by string courses. Blind arcading began as an interior feature, but soon extended to the exterior of churches, where the pilasters were eventually separated from the exterior walls for a new effect.

Much of the sculpture in Romanesque churches was painted after it was completed. Monumental paintings also covered interior church walls. Only fragments of them survive, but they show that the painting of the day imitated sculptural styles and manuscript illuminations. The interior of the Church of Notre Dame La Grande at Poitiers is decorated with painted patterns. It serves as a reminder that many of the great Romanesque churches, despite their dark, ponderous mass, were once radiant with color and reflected light.

The Romanesque style was at its height between 1075 and 1125 in France, Britain, and Germany. The style never won general acceptance in Italy, though some Romanesque churches can be seen there. This era of church-building produced a new generation of itinerant, skilled masons and craftsman, who, in 1140, turned their skills to the construction of the first Gothic cathedral, at St.-Denis.

LEFT: The leaning tower of Pisa is the cathedral of Pisa's free-standing belfry. It is decorated with the miniature arcading of translucent marble—a decorative motif in Tuscan Romanesque and Gothic architecture. *Pisa, Italy.*

RIGHT: Tuscan architects of the middle ages were inspired by their proximity to classical antiquity, decorating the exteriors of their churches with slender ranks of marble columns and blind arcades. Statues of saints were prominently placed on the church gable, as St. Michael is here over the ornately decorated façade of his church. *Church of San Michelle, Lucca, Italy.*

CHAPTER TWO

THE RISE OF THE GOTHIC CATHEDRAL

In 1140, Abbot Suger's intention to increase the light in the Benedictine church of St.- Denis near Paris created a new style of architecture. It became Suger's ambition to create the most beautiful church of his time, and he required the talents of France's greatest painters, sculptors, and metalworkers. The remade abbey church at St.-Denis exemplifies the elemental delicacy and beauty of the Gothic cathedral. By 1150, the cathedrals of Noyon and Sensils were begun. Notre-Dame in Paris would follow in 1163.

If the pendentive dome of the Hagia Sophia brought heaven down to earth, the soaring height of the Gothic cathedral's spires and transparency of its windows lifted the spirit heavenward. To many, the Gothic cathedral is the architectural realization of man's desire to be near God. The cathedral was most certainly the dominant art form of the Gothic era.

The awe-inspiring height of the Gothic cathedral and its slender delicacy was achieved by a new mastery of the pointed arch. The height of a round arch depended upon its span, but the span of a pointed arch could be varied to almost any degree. The pointed arch solved the problems of imperfectly balanced stone vaulting; massive load-bearing walls were no longer necessary.

The introduction of the rib vault and the use of the pointed arch introduced diagonal and transverse ribs into the structure of stone church ceilings. This new use of the diagonal rib and pointed arch allowed the weight of the vault to be concentrated at particular points, from which the thrust could be transferred to the buttresses supporting the outer walls of the building.

Vaultings

Rib vaulting outlined the edges of the stone vault and concealed the irregular curves of the groin, or edge, of the vault. Ribs divided space, and patterns of vaultings, which began purely as structural elements, soon became one of the major aesthetic elements of the Gothic style. The division of rectangular bays into three, four, or six sections lent even more variety with the introduction of the ridge rib.

The ridge rib was a horizontal line that extended from the crown of the vault. This rib, which cut only the surface of the vault, increased the variety of geometric and decorative patterns of vaulting, and gave unity to divided vaults. In the cathedral at Montivilliers near Le Havre, the ridge rib extends along the entire nave and appears to make one bay melt into another.

RIGHT: The eleventh-century Romanesque church of St. Jacques was converted to a Gothic Cathedral in 1538. The church's magnificent stone vaultings are characteristic of the late Gothic, when vaultings became almost purely decorative. The high nave is illuminated by the clerestory windows. *Eglise St. Jacques, Liège, Belgium.*

LEFT: Notre-Dame was begun in 1163, and was under construction for 170 years. It became one of the most copied of the early Gothic cathedrals. Badly damaged during the French Revolution, work to restore the cathedral's interior and exterior began in 1845 after the publication of Victor Hugo's novel *The Hunchback of Notre Dame. Paris, France.*

BELOW: Sculpture in portals was seen by arriving and departing worshipers, which made them favored locations for sculptures. Portal compositions coupled the lessons of the New and Old Testaments, and glorified Christ, The Virgin, and the saints. Shown here is the south portal of Rouen Cathedral. *Rouen, France.*

At Exeter and Lincoln cathedrals, in England, the ridge rib unifies the dramatic, upward-thrusting "palm" vaulting.

The use of vaulting became more spectacular and the patterns became more fantastic as architects experimented with form, as with the octagon in the dome which replaced a collapsed tower in Ely Cathedral. Decorative vaulting at its most elaborate and most English can be seen in the fan vaulting at King's College Chapel in Cambridge and in the cloister of Gloucester Cathedral. Vaulting often endowed a cathedral with much of its grace, and played a large part in the emotional impact of the architecture on the worshiper.

Church ceilings soared with new freedom. More and more, the spaces in between the vaultings could be given over to the windows of extraordinary height and color which would imbue the nave of the Gothic cathedral with its devotional atmosphere.

Stained Glass and Tracery

Stained glass was the translucent art form of the West. Even the lead that outlined and held together the pattern of colored glass in church windows served as part of the window's design. Colored glass was used like the precious stones encrusting the caskets of reliquaries, and it made the cathedral a treasure-house of spirituality.

Few early stained-glass windows survive. Those that do show a subdued and less brilliant use of color. (The supreme example of the use of jewel-like light is the lavish, but small, church of Sainte-Chapelle in Paris, built by Louis the Pious to house a sacred relic—Christ's crown of thorns.)

Early Gothic windows were narrow, pointed arches. As the Gothic style was perfected, the stone supports became more and more slender, and the space for decorated glass increased. Stone tracery was developed to divide the windows and give them strength.

LEFT: A crown of thorns decorates the pinnacles of the Sainte-Chapelle, but it is the transparency of the upper chapel that makes it seem like a church without walls. Fifteen stained-glass windows, separated by the narrowest of columns, fill Saint Louis' chapel with "gothic light." *Paris, France.*

RIGHT: The establishment of Canterbury Cathedral dates back to the arrival of Augustine, the church's first archbishop, in 697. It was rebuilt in 1178 following a fire, and became England's first Gothic Cathedral. *Kent, England.*

RIGHT: The soaring nave of Sint-Bavokerk was completed in 1550. The church itself became a favorite subject of the Haarlem School artists during the seventeenth century. Its famous, ornate Baroque organ— beloved by composers such as Handel and Mozart— is the centerpiece of the Gothic church's interior. *St. Bavokerk. Haarlem, Netherlands.*

RIGHT: Shown here is the extraordinary center doorway tympanum at the thirteenth-century St. Servaaskerk in Maastricht, Netherlands.

LEFT: When the township of Leiden became the profitable center of the Dutch weaving industry in the fourteenth century, it financed the construction of a Gothic church, St. Pancraskerk. The church nave, adorned with star vaulting, has the unusual distinction of being lower than the transept and choir. *St. Pancraskerk, Leiden, Netherlands.*

LEFT: King Louis IX commissioned the building of the Sainte-Chapelle in 1248 as a reliquary for Christ's crown of thorns. The lower chapel, where servants and commoners worshipped, is shown here. The King and the royal family worshipped in the upper chapel. *Paris, France.*

At first, plate tracery—in which stone plates were joined to the masonry on either side of the window by holes pierced in the wall—was employed. The introduction of bar tracery gave the windows greater strength and enhanced the narrative possibilities of colored glass, allowing master glassmakers to use a series of medallions to recapitulate Christ's lessons and the lives of the saints.

The expertise of the glassmakers matured with the skill of stonemasons. Circles, lozenges, quatrefoils, and squares were fashioned in the iron armature that served as a medallion's framework. The result was a skillful display of light and color that astonished the worshipers with its splendor, and instructed them in the teachings important to Christian life.

The ribbed fretwork of bar tracery soon spread to decorate screens, blind arches, vaults, canopies, and tombs. Decorative importance was also given to structural features such as buttresses, piers, vaulting ribs, shafts, and gables. A new naturalism was employed in the sculpted ornamentation of tracery. Naturalistic foliage and flowers began to be used extensively in carving during the thirteenth century, and was transformed into an upward-climbing mass of leaves and vines on the capitals of columns, on moldings, and on pulpits.

Rose windows, circular windows filled with stone tracery, gradually became one of the essential elements of design of the Gothic cathedral. They originated from circular windows representing the Wheel of Fortune, in which the tracery serves as spokes on a wheel. In the cathedrals at Reims and Strasbourg, the pattern of the tracery spreads like a flower, with pointed petals lying in a circle.

LEFT: The stained-glass windows and thousands of scuptures decorating Chartres Cathedal make a monumental encyclopedia of the beliefs, hope, and learning of the middle ages. It was Abbot Suger's idea that each bit of sculpture should have a place in the vast stone drama, so everyone could study the Gospels.

Rose windows were usually part of the western entrance of the church; their circular shape became an integral part of the design of the western façade, and of the church itself. The light through the rose window shines toward the altar, illuminating the worshiper's steps into the nave, and conveying the comforting essence of the Virgin to the returning worshiper through a rainbow of light.

RIGHT: Light had mystical force in the medieval church. Gothic tracery, made up of separately fashioned jambs, bars, circular forms, and spheroids, made possible the evanescent light of the Gothic cathedral. Shown here is the darkly-colored rose window at Reims. *Reims, France.*

LEFT: Shown here are the magnificent north transept rose and lancet windows of Chartres Cathedral in France. The lancet windows tell the biblical stories of Melchizedek and Nebuchadnezzer, David and Saul, St. Anne, Solomon, Herod, and Aaron and Pharaoh.

Exterior Changes

The changes to the exteriors of church buildings were as profound as those to the interiors. The naturally radiating lines of the flying buttresses accentuated the vertical lines of the towers and spires, while the sloping arches of the flying buttresses balanced vertical and horizontal lines and framed the monumental portals of the west entrances of Laon and Notre-Dame. Later cathedrals, such as Chartres, Amiens, and Reims, competed to be the churches with the highest vaults and spires.

With the beginning of the nave and the choir of Chartres Cathedral in 1194, mastery replaced experimentation in French Gothic architecture. The west portals of Chartres show the new power of figural sculpture and the blending of sculpture with architectural lines. Craftsmen throughout Europe, as well as those who traveled with the Crusaders to rebuild the churches of the Holy Land, began to emulate the graceful arches and decoration of the French Gothic cathedral.

RIGHT: The flying buttresses on the side of St. Maclou, Rouen, were constructed in the fifteenth century. They are given a delicacy by the Flamboyant-style ornamentation of pinnacles and Gothic arches. *St. Maclou, Rouen, France.*

BELOW: The pinnacled pink-and-white marble façade of the Milan Cathedral shows that it is one of the few Italian Gothic churches to be influenced by French Gothic. Begun in 1387, it was not finished until 1858. *Milan, Italy.*

ABOVE: Reims is the cathedral where the monarchs of France were traditionally consecrated. It was to Reims that Joan of Arc brought Charles VII to be crowned. The pure form of the filigree-like bar tracery of the Gothic cathedral was first created at Reims, and can be seen above the statuary in the rose window. *Reims, France.*

RIGHT: Amiens Cathedral represents the high point of French Gothic architecture. It was begun in 1220 to house the head of John the Baptist brought back from the Holy Land in 1206 by French crusaders. The abundant decoration of the western and southern façades was called "almost encyclopedic" by John Ruskin. *Amiens, France.*

ABOVE: Buttresses were necessary to shore up the tall walls of the Gothic cathedral. Architects tried to disguise their essential function by decorating them and making them part of the design of the church's exterior. Shown here is a thirteenth-century buttress at Chartes Cathedral.

RIGHT: *Salisbury Cathedral from the Bishop's Grounds* by John Constable, 1823. The towers and spires of English Gothic cathedrals were slender and exceptionally graceful. The 404-foot (123-meter) spire of Salisbury Cathedral was completed at the end of the thirteenth century, and is the tallest in England. *Wiltshire, England.*

ABOVE: Exeter Cathedral, completed in 1369, is one of the finest Gothic cathedrals in the English Decorated style.
Its stylistic innovation was to use the entire façade as a vast screen to hold statues of the saints. *Exeter, England.*

The Transmission of the Gothic Style

The development of the Gothic style in England mimicked its evolution in France. In 1174, the French architect William Sens was brought to Canterbury to reconstruct the cathedral after a fire destroyed part of it. Sens died before the cathedral was completed, but the Gothic style had arrived in England. The completed cathedral at Canterbury was as emulated throughout England as the abbey church of St.-Denis was in France.

Towers and exterior decoration became more elaborate and intricate. The use of marble in columns and arcades gave a lavish simplicity to the interior of some English cathedrals and parish churches. The final phase of the high Gothic in England was dubbed the "perpendicular," and it enlarged the use of glass over stone. English church interiors of this period, such as Kings College at Cambridge, display the great English innovation of elaborate fan vaulting.

The Gothic style was introduced to Spain by monks from the south of France in the thirteenth century. It arrived in Toledo, León, and Bourgos as a mature import. Bourgos, Spain's first Gothic cathedral, was begun in 1221 as a defiant symbol of Christianity, and it served as an inspiration for the reconquest of the Moorish peninsula.

The Cathedral of Seville was constructed over the site of a mosque, and its bell tower covers the minaret. Moorish influences were soon evident in Spanish Gothic constructions, especially in the interior decoration, which combined rhythmic Islamic design with Romanesque and Gothic arcades. Window sizes were reduced, increasing the height of the pier arcades and omitting the triforium. In its later phase, with its soaring vaults and towers, Spanish Gothic became a true architecture of exuberance.

BELOW: Fan vaulting was the last great innovation of the English Decorated style. It can be seen here at King's College Chapel in Cambridge. This picture also shows the chapel's great organ as it appears to visitors entering the church. *Cambridge, England.*

LEFT: The rebuilding of Westminster Abbey began in 1220 under the direction of Henry III, who admired the cathedrals of Reims and Amiens and the Sainte-Chapelle. With the exception of the west towers which were added by Hawksmoor in the eighteenth century, the church was completed with remarkable unity of style in 1532. *London, England.*

ABOVE: Begun as a shrine to Henry the VI in 1503, this beautiful chapel was ordered to be "painted, garnished and adorned in as goodly and rich a manner as such work requireth and as to a king's work apperteyneth" by Henry VII. Known as the Chapel of Henry VII, it is one of the finest examples of late English Gothic. *London, England.*

RIGHT: Cologne was transformed into a holy city when the relics of the Three Magi were transferred there from Milan in 1164. The Cathedral was built to house them. Based on the Cathedral at Reims, Cologne was begun in 1248. It is largely a medieval structure, but it was not completed until the nineteenth century. *Cologne, Germany.*

RIGHT: Gargoyles were first used on the exterior of cathedrals to ward off evil. At Notre-Dame in Paris they hide behind the large upper gallery between the towers. They were later given a functional use as well—as water spouts. The creatures shown here are from Cologne Cathedral in Germany.

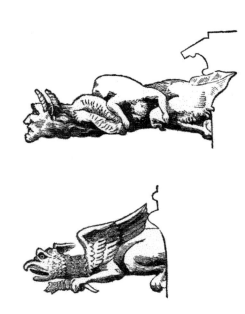

ABOVE: Stone tracery grew more decorative as simple plate tracery was replaced by bar tracery that enabled windows to become larger. Tracery became so thin in the late Flamboyant style that the stone was reinforced with iron. Shown here is a German fish-bladder tracery pattern. *Stuttgart, Germany.*

The Late Gothic Style in Germany

The Gothic style in Germany did not take hold until the thirteenth century. The German Gothic cathedral retained the massive bulk of the Romanesque and exploited the picturesque use of spires and towers. The same striving for height and lightness is evident in Cologne (1248) and Beauvais, begun in 1247.

The sense of proportion is vital to all Gothic cathedrals. European architects devoted enormous energy to rendering in stone what they believed was the majesty of God and the order of his creation. In striving to reach these heights of expression and altitude, architects sometimes went too far, for the vault of the Beauvais Cathedral collapsed soon after it was built.

Germany's special contribution to Gothic architecture was the hall church, a rectangular building, usually without transepts. The structure's emphasis on the horizontal lead to a new treatment of space in late Gothic churches. One such hall-church building, in Freiburg in Saxony (1484), is considered one of the most perfect realizations of the meeting of the horizontal and vertical. The octagonal piers in this hall-church have concave sides, and the vault of the nave is not separated from the side aisles by arches, but runs through the nave to the chapels. The church's tulip pulpit, designed in 1500, is covered with growing vegetable forms that carry the eye upward.

The Germans excelled in the picturesque use of the spire. Beginning with the tower at Freiburg im Breisgau, Gothic spires allowed the interior and exterior to merge, unlike Romanesque towers, which had been closed. The originality and technical expertise of Strasbourg Cathedral's turrets and spires earned it a reputation as the eighth wonder of the world. One can climb the outside of the spire and be in the church at the same time, earning it the distinction of being the "most Gothic" of all spires.

The Gothic style in Italy was tempered by the classical proportions of the architecture of the Roman Empire, and it never

BELOW: St. Stephen's Cathedral in Vienna was begun in the fourteenth century when the Gothic style had reached its full maturity. Its distinctive roof is made up of almost a quarter of a million glazed tiles. *Vienna, Austria.*

achieved the verticality of the Gothic in Northern Europe. The Italian skill in fresco painting, coupled with the need for small windows in the Mediterranean climate, prevented the development of interest in stained glass. Marble and brick, not limestone, were the materials of the Italian churches. The surface decoration consisted of flat, polychromatic patterns that enhanced the marble's translucency.

The late stages of the high Gothic style, such as French Rayonnant, Flamboyant, and English Decorated, grew more and more ornate. The term "Gothic" was first used disparagingly by eighteenth-century critics of the architecture of the middle ages, but by the beginning of the nineteenth century, the Gothic style was better understood, and Gothic architecture was seen as a style of continuous growth and freedom. Shaped by the taste of the clergy's and aristocracy's elite, it represented the technical and artistic achievement of accomplished lay master craftsmen. Above all, it is considered today to be the representative art form of the "Age of Faith."

LEFT: Emmanuel de Witte's *Interior of the Oude Kerk (Old Church) at Amsterdam* depicts typical worshippers in the seventeenth century, including one family who has brought their dog to church.

RIGHT: The façade of Siena Cathedral, begun c. 1226, is distinctly classical, setting the stage for the decorative saints, prophets, and philosophers addressing each other and the passer-bys below.

CHAPTER THREE

RENAISSANCE AND BAROQUE ARCHITECTURE

The exact date of the cultural Renaissance is sometimes disputed, but it is safe to say that the Renaissance of classical architecture began in Florence in 1420 with the construction of Florence Cathedral. The architect was Filippo Brunelleschi, who made an intensive study of vaulting methods used in imperial Roman buildings such as the Pantheon.

Brunelleschi used contemporary—Gothic—and ancient construction methods to construct the wide dome of Florence Cathedral. The pointed dome was built in the Gothic manner with slender ribs and a light double vault. Inspired by the techniques of the ancient Romans, Brunelleschi used herringbone brickwork for greater strength. The dome was not finished until after the architect's death in 1446, but it revived the use of ancient Roman forms for church-building.

ABOVE: The doors of the Baptistry of Florence Cathedral were called "The Gates of Paradise" by Michelangelo. Designed by Lorenzo Ghiberti in 1425, they became the artist's life work. The panels depicting dramatic scenes from the Old Testament took more than twenty years to complete. *Florence, Italy.*

LEFT: The Jesuits refurbished the interiors of many churches in Austria and Bavaria during the Counter Reformation. They also built churches to celebrate their "victory over Protestantism." Many of them are jewels of Baroque art. Here we see the twin towers of the Hopfgarten *Tirol, Austria.*

LEFT: This Gothic church, Santa Maria Novella, was given a Renaissance façade designed by Alberti in 1458. *Florence, Italy.*

St. Peter's Basilica

In 1447, Pope Nicholas V decided to rebuild Old St. Peter's in Rome. It was his ambition to restore Rome's former imperial glory through the grandeur of its architecture, and St. Peter's and the Roman Catholic Church would be at the heart of the rebuilt city.

Pope Nicholas ordered the new building to be built around the old basilica. The architect and sculptor Bernardo Rossellino began the construction of the new church, but work on St. Peter's was discontinued at Nicholas' death. It was not resumed until 1503 under the pontificate of Julius II, who had in his employment three masters—Bramante, Raphael, and Michelangelo.

When work on St. Peter's resumed, both Constantinople and Jerusalem were in Islamic hands. The two great churches of antiquity, the Hagia Sophia and the Holy Sepulchre in Jerusalem, were lost, and Rome was to take Constantinople's place as God's divine city.

The new St. Peter's was to be a colossal martyrium, and the old basilica was to be torn down. The work took over a century to complete. The conception was Bramante's. His design—based on a Greek cross—was converted into a Latin cross to

LEFT: This picture of Maderno's façade of St. Peter's Church captures the grandeur of the colossal statues of Christ and His Apostles. Christ's arm is raised in blessing and in celebration of the triumph of the aesthetic of the Italian Renaissance. *Vatican City, Rome, Italy.*

RIGHT: Shown here is the coffered ceiling and arches of St. Peter's Basilica with part of the cathedral's magnificent dome. The detailed attention to decoration contributes to the effect of balance, symmetry, and calm majesty. *St. Peter's, Rome, Italy.*

RIGHT: Smolny Cathedral in St. Petersburg is a rare example of Italian Baroque architecture with its delicate twin towers and gently curving concave façades wedded to the domed Greek cross plan of the Russian Orthodox Church. *St. Petersburg, Russia.*

FOLLOWING PAGE: The *Wieskirche* ("Meadow Church") is one of the most ornate Rococo churches. It became the center of pilgrimage in 1730 when a farmer found a weeping statue of the scourged Jesus, and, afterward, the church built a religious palace around the site. *Wies, Germany.*

accommodate a greater number of worshipers and pilgrims. Raphael, Peruzzi, and Antonio da Sangallo succeeded Bramante. Their task was a formidable one. None of the men had worked on a structure of this size before. After Bramante's death, work was suspended again.

In 1546, Pope Paul III assigned Michelangelo to succeed Sangallo. Michelangelo was seventy-two years old; he would work on the completion of St. Peter's until his death in 1564 at the age of eighty-nine. Michelangelo's plan for the interior underneath the dome preserved the original centralized space of Bramante's design and opened the floor pattern at the corners, creating a single, integrated cross and square that unified the interior.

At the time of Michelangelo's death, most of the central part of the church had been finished. The spacious central dome was still incomplete, but the completion of the new church was assured. St. Peter's is not solely Michelangelo's conception, but the sculptor is credited with the human effect of the gigantic structure.

The final stage of St. Peters' construction was begun in 1629 when Gianlorenzo Bernini became the architect. His contribution to the awe-inspiring effect of St. Peter's is as powerful as Michelangelo's humanist touch. Bernini constructed the dramatic oval colonnades decorated with huge sculptures of Christ and his Apostles that surround the entrance. The colonnades

LEFT: The parish Church of St. Michael in Peiting has a Romanesque tower and crypt, and a Rococo pulpit and high altar. This picture shows the elegant use of curved and concave lines favored by Baroque architects for their ability to create spatial illusions. The undulating lines of the balcony are echoed in the winged ornamentation on the pews. *St. Michael, Pieting, Germany.*

BELOW: Baroque architects sought to create a complete environment, using the space around or leading to public buildings to new and dramatic effect. This aerial view of the Piazza San Pietro shows how Bernini's huge oval colonnade magnifies St. Peter's eminence. *Rome, Italy.*

and the central point of the magnificent piazza, the Egyptian obelisk, enhance the eminence of the basilica and complete St. Peter's. Bernini's low, wide colonnade was constructed so that it would not obscure anyone's view of the Pope. It intensified the *theater sacrum* of the basilica—and it was Baroque.

Baroque Architecture

"Baroque" was first used as a term of abuse for something convoluted or misshapen. Baroque architecture first developed in Rome in the early seventeenth century among Bernini's

contemporaries—Bernini, Francesco Borromini, Pietro da Cortona, and Guarino Guarini. These architects experimented with central oval designs, concave façades, convex porches, and interior curved balconies.

The use of the curved form produced an illusion of movement and allowed architects to use space, especially that of the interior of a church, in such a way that reality would seem to slip away as the worshiper entered the nave or confronted the revelation of the altar.

Architecture, sculpture, and painting merged in the Baroque period. Within Baroque architecture, the stress on classic proportion relaxed and was replaced by a new pictorial emphasis. Columns and pilasters became purely decorative. Sculpture was used to adorn window frames, capitals, balustrades, and finials. Special attention was given to the setting and grouping of buildings; when possible, the surrounding terrain was designed with an impressive approach, including terraces, esplanades, and flights of steps. The Bom Jesús in Portugal, standing at the pinnacle of a cascading flight of steps and fountains, is one such example of the dramatic use of the environment.

Baroque church architecture is overwhelmingly Catholic, and is associated with the Counter-Reformation launched by the Catholic Church in response to the Protestant Reformation. It flourished in Italy, Portugal, Spain, and Flanders, as well as Austria, southern Germany, and Bavaria, where many churches, refurbished during the eighteenth century, incorporated the drama of Baroque art and the pastels and dainty groupings that became known as Rococo.

The Baroque employed every art and illusion to transport the Catholic worshiper into a visionary world. The ornamentation of the Baroque church is excessively lavish and sensual, seeking to astonish and overwhelm the worshiper.

BELOW: The Santa Maria della Salute, begun in 1631 and finished over fifty years later, was built in thanks for the city's deliverance from the plague which claimed forty thousand lives in Venice. The dome of the church is supported by huge scrolls, which make up the base of the church's sculpted crown for the Virgin, who is worshipped here as "The Ruler of the Sea." *Venice, Italy.*

ABOVE: Sint-Michielskerk was constructed between 1650 and 1666 by Willem Hesius in Leuven. The triumphant figures on the Baroque church's façade became almost ubiquitous on the altars and in the decoration of Baroque churches in the Low Countries and in Bavaria and Austria. *St. Michael's Church, Leuven, Belgium.*

LEFT: The Benedictine Abbey of Melk is one of the pilgrimage churches of Austria. It made use of Rococo and Baroque styles and colors to stun the senses of visiting pilgrims. *Melk, Austria.*

The Spanish Baroque Style

Spanish architects and sculptors brought an exultant energy to the façades and interiors of their churches. Spain was a conservative, Catholic nation, still triumphant from the conquest of the Moors in Granada in 1492. Spanish church architects and sculptors used the dramatic art of the Baroque to infuse the individual with the religious power of the Church. Decoration of churches achieved bewildering richness, and sculpture and painting achieved new vitality to an overwhelming effect.

Spanish builders had adopted decorative motifs of the Italian Renaissance—putti, medallions, grotesque swags, garlands of flowers, and fruit—with a remarkable understanding of their decorative values. This style became known as Plateresque, because the artists were described as *plateros en yeso*—silversmiths in stucco.

By the mid-sixteenth century, Spanish architects and artists were carrying the curved lines and pictorial emphasis of Baroque church architecture to extravagant extremes. The most fantastic of these styles was called Churrigueresque; the sacristy of the Charterhouse in Granada, Spain, exemplifies the style associated with the Churriguera family. Every pilaster, capital, and cornice contributes to a fever of lines and curves.

The art of the Baroque and the Rococo was one of high contrast. It lent itself amazingly well to the fusion of two civilizations which were, in some ways, the antithesis of each other.

The Baroque in the Americas

The friars who arrived with the Spanish and Portuguese conquistadors in South and Middle America in the early sixteenth century encountered remarkable civilizations very different

LEFT: This façade of the Church of Santa Cruz shows the Spanish use of classical ornamental motifs employed to lavish decorative effect on façades and interiors. *Seville, Spain.*

from their own—civilizations in which Christianity had no significance. Yet, before the Spanish conquest was a century old, ambitious and spacious churches were under construction in the New World. The planning was carried out by a handful of ecclesiastics, but most of the labor was accomplished by natives.

In 1556, the Dominican archbishop Alonso de Montufar wrote to Phillip II describing the work on Mexican monasteries, which he claimed were so grand that they were worthy of the Spanish city of Valladolid. The archbishop wrote of crews of five hundred to a thousand natives called up to work on the monastery's construction without wages or even food, only as an act of faith.

RIGHT: Mission Santa Barbara was established in 1786; the church that now stands on the site was completed in 1820. The squarish twin bell towers are typical of the California missions, but the façade is not. *Santa Barbara, California.*

LEFT: The foundation for the Rococo towers and Plateresque façade of Mission Dolores was established in 1776 by a small group of Franciscan friars and settlers who hoped to find a better life in this Spanish settlement. *San Francisco, California.*

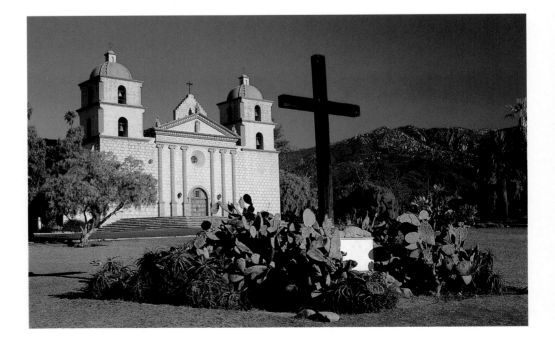

RIGHT: The decoration of the Baroque church used every device of art and illusion to transport the worshipper into a mystical realm, and to glorify the saints and magnify the supremacy of the Catholic Church. *Altar, Abbey of Melk, Melk, Austria.*

LEFT: The tall tower of the Westerkerk, a mixture of Baroque and Gothic styles, dominates Amsterdam's Prinsengracht Canal. The church was begun in 1620, after Amsterdam adopted Protestantism as its principal faith. *Westerkerk, Amsterdam, Netherlands.*

RIGHT: The Dominican monastery in San Cristóbal de las Casas was founded in 1545 after the arrival of the first friar, but the church probably was not finished until 1700. Its façade is remarkably high and original and uses a lace-like pattern. *San Cristóbal, Chiapas, Mexico.*

How free this act of faith was can be disputed. What is indisputable is the skill that native artists brought to copying Spanish church art and inventing their own. Faith—first used to subjugate a conquered people—was re-created by the hands of indigenous craftsmen, who produced a form of church decoration that was in sympathy and at one with the lives of the poor in the midst of ornate glory.

Baroque art in Latin America incorporated the Indian's sense of form and color, along with his world view, into pained images of suffering. This art was most strikingly original and powerful in the areas which were the foundation of pre-Columbian capitals—Mexico City, Quito in Ecuador, and Cuzco and Lima in Peru.

Churches and Cathedrals in the Americas

The colonial church was often modest, but the colonial cathedral was imposing, set on a stepped platform above the level of the plaza before it. (The Cathedral of Mexico City is built over the site of an Aztec temple, and constructed from the temple's stones.) Decoration was lavished on the church façade. Three entrances were usual, and two towers served as belfries and buttressed the sides.

In the grander buildings, the choir occupied part of the central area of the nave, just as it did in Spanish cathedrals. It was enclosed on three sides, and faced the main altar. Choir stalls, organs, coffered ceilings, and pulpits all lent themselves to lavish ornamentation, and all displayed the art of native painters and wood-carvers. The silver of Mexico and the gold of Colombia and Ecuador added additional richness to ornate altars and ceilings. Indigenous flora and fauna such as palm leaves, fruits, and

seashells found their way into church sculpture and decoration.

Lima, Cuzco, Quito, and San Domingo all contain churches with amazing interior beauty. The Incas produced some of the finest masonry ever seen, and the façades of São Francisco and San Augustin in Lima are densely decorated. These churches have a massive quality that has nothing to do with their actual size; large masonry blocks were used in their construction, to protect against earthquake damage.

The Baroque period reached its maturity in the decoration of the Cathedral of Mexico City. Here, the lavishness of the Spanish Baroque and Churrigueresque styles is elaborated and modified by the Mestizo style, born in the masonry workshops of the Aztecs. The fantastic decoration of the façade incorporates many Aztec features and uses many Indian faces. The confluence of the artistic heritage of the two different cultures has created a passionate church art of dizzying vitality and originality. Construction of the cathedral was begun in 1525. It was rebuilt in 1573, and was enlarged periodically until 1813. It is the largest and oldest cathedral in Latin America, and it houses the "Black Christ," a miracle-working carving of the Crucifixion.

The Cult of Saints

Sculpted, modeled, and painted images of the saints were used in festivals and in churches for their storytelling power. Many images are of founders of religious orders, such as St. Ignatius of Loyola, the founder of the Jesuits, and St. Francis of Assisi, the patron saint and founder of the Franciscan order.

What is moving about these images is their quiet nobility amid the frenzy of decoration. Angels have Indian faces, while saints and prophets look like suffering peasants, or very like the

RIGHT: The Cathedral of Mexico City was built on the site of an Aztec temple using the temple stones. It was begun on a massive scale in 1573, and was completed nearly a hundred years later.

The decoration on the façade of the Sagrario Metropolitano, on the far right, has the details of the decoration of the Sacristy at Granada and has been called "ultra baroque." *Mexico City, Mexico.*

LEFT: The Sanctuary of Ocotlán is located on a hill where the palace of an Indian ruler is said to have stood. The church dates from 1745. The interior was finished in the mid-nineteenth century, and the gilding continued into the 1940s. *Oaxaca, Mexico.*

native craftsmen with a high indigenous artistic culture and the indifference of Portugal to her colony during the sixteenth century are responsible for the simplicity of the early churches.

A luscious Rococo style developed in the coastal churches, such as those in Pernambuco, Recife. The city is situated on a great elbow of land, the nearest point in the New World to the Old. In colonial times, ships arrived there weeks before they arrived in Rio de Janeiro. Recife is home to sixty-two churches, many Baroque masterpieces. The Church of São Pedro dos Clérigos, with slender towers and many windows, is among them.

With the seventeenth-century discovery of gold and diamonds and exploitation of the mines in the mountains, the Baroque and Rococo styles began to flourish in Brazilian church architecture, especially in the inland captaincy of Minas Gerais, and church societies competed with each other in erecting and adorning their churches. The church of São Francisco at Ouro Preto is located in the center of the mining district. It was built by Antonio Francisco Lisboa, known as *El Aleijadinho* ("The Little Cripple"), who, like the Italian masters of the Baroque, was an architect and a sculptor. The decorated façade of the church is unusual in that it has round towers. Because of an abundance of exceptionally hard woods, few of these churches are vaulted; the local quartz also made structural and aesthetic contributions.

Brazil's most famous Baroque church is the basilica of Bom Jesús de Matozinhos in Congouhas do Compo. The Bom Jesús is also the work of the architect Antonio Francisco Lisboa. Its façade has the sculptural quality of European high Baroque.

The Late Baroque

Spain and Portugal were not the only countries colonizing the New World: The Dutch and French had established their own settlements, and the English were colonizing the eastern seaboard of North America while the Spanish explorer Juan Ponce de León discovered Florida during his disappointing search for the fabled fountain of youth.

In Europe, the late Baroque style merged into a new, sober style called Neoclassicism; this convergence can be seen in the work of the English architect Sir Christopher Wren. Wren's churches had an enormous influence on Protestant architecture in the thirteen English colonies which would become the United States.

Europeans with gaunt, pained, or beatific faces. The representations of Christ show a man bent over with suffering. Some images, like that of the "Black Christ" and the painting of the Virgin of Guadeloupe, which occupies a chapel of its own in the Cathedral of Sucre in Bolivia, became famous when miraculous powers were attributed to them. But while these images may be famous, they are not unique in the Americas, where remarkable powers of healing and the gift of spiritual comfort are attributed to representations of the saints and the Virgin Mary.

Brazil's Churches

Brazil's early churches were simple structures. The Portuguese colonists had experience with violent earthquakes and did not construct churches with vaulted domes and towers. The lack of

CHAPTER FOUR

GEORGIAN AND ROMAN REVIVAL CHURCHES

There was almost no church-building in England from the time of Henry VIII's separation of the Anglican and Catholic Churches in 1534 until the Great Fire of London in 1666. The task of rebuilding the great medieval city was a tremendous one; King Charles II assigned the rebuilding of London's churches to the city's assistant surveyor-general, Sir Christopher Wren.

Why King Charles chose Wren is not clear. Wren had little architectural experience; he was a scientist and professor of astronomy. And Charles had earlier rejected Wren's ambitious scheme to rebuild London on formal, geometric lines—a plan in which public buildings were to be constructed on spacious piazzas and linked by wide avenues.

LEFT: The nave of St. Paul's integrates the grandeur of the great classical churches of antiquity with a Baroque love of sculptural illusion. Supporting structures are artfully disguised, as are the great piers under the central dome on which the arches are outlined to make it appear that the crossing space is an octagon. *London, England.*

Wren's geometric placement of churches in the "new London" disregarded the sites of the destroyed churches, showing no respect for parish boundaries. London had to be rebuilt as quickly as possible, but landowners and merchants preferred to rebuild the medieval city rather than remake it with Wren's broad avenues.

Despite the plan's impracticality, Charles entrusted Wren with the rebuilding of fifty-two London churches, including St. Paul's Cathedral. Wren proved to be a brilliant choice. The young assistant surveyor experimented with Gothic and Neoclassical architectural forms simultaneously. In the process, he created a new style of Protestant architecture that combined the portico of a columned temple with a Gothic spire.

Wren's towers and steeples were Gothic cathedral spires reinterpreted using Roman forms. No two churches are alike, but the general pattern is that of a lofty, square tower, surmounted by upper stories of diminishing size and topped by a needle-like spire. Just enough curvilinear detail from the Baroque was added to enliven the designs while preserving the Protestant preference for reserved simplicity.

The original sites of most of the London churches were small, and often irregular. Churches had been hemmed in by surrounding buildings in the old medieval city, as they would

LEFT: St. Paul's Cathedral is Christopher Wren's Baroque masterpiece. It is not typical of his other steepled churches, or of any other Baroque structure. St. Paul's huge dome was designed to make it part of a distant vista of a city full of steepled churches. *London, England.*

be again. Wren decided to give particular emphasis to towers, and he remade London as a city of steepled churches.

Neoclassicism in the hands of Wren and his associates, especially Nicholas Hawksmoor, became the basis for a style that has been called "refreshingly undoctrinaire." (Hawksmoor used the style with particularly original effect in his London parish churches.) Neoclassicism was eclectic: It blended the portico of an ancient temple with the medieval church spire in a work of surprising grace.

Wren had no formal school of followers, but he had many admirers and imitators. Skilled architects and carpenters were able to reproduce his simple, clean designs. The modesty and economy of his small English churches perfectly suited the needs of the American colonists in the early eighteenth century.

The Churches of New England

The first buildings in New England were medieval in style, very much like the old churches and houses in the villages of England's East Anglia, from which many of the first colonists emigrated. The Protestant Episcopal Church of Old Trinity, in Church Creek, Maryland, is one such building. Erected in 1674, the brick church is built along the lines of a small cottage with one apsidal end.

It was some time before colonists were established enough to attempt a more elegant design. The tradition of the seventeenth-century Protestant "four-square" meetinghouse lingered into the eighteenth century. Churches were often plain, barn-like, clapboard structures with a side entrance and no tower or spire. When congregations were at last able to imitate English models, their churches developed an individual style which became distinctly American.

This was partly because of the difference in building materials. In many areas stone was rare, and brick and limestone were largely unavailable. The churches of the American colonies were made of wood. In fact, wood became the preferred material of construction in the fledgling and heavily forested United States. It was "good to live in a house of wood"—a belief that made Thomas Jefferson complain that there was a prejudice against brick and stone.

Wood was the major contributor to the colonial church's distinctive look. The wooden columns on classical porticos were slender and more graceful than those of stone, and the exteriors were often shingled.

In the eighteenth century, when congregations were wealthy and established enough to consider rebuilding their churches, they looked not only to Wren's designs, but also to those of

RIGHT: The Greek Revival in architecture was largely confined to the construction of public and government buildings, but this church at the University of Georgia, Athens, has taken its inspiration from the Parthenon. *Athens, Georgia.*

ABOVE: The formula of portico and steeple was a simple one, but it is elegant in this Georgian-styled, wooden, colonial church. The classical columns are gone, and reveal the clean lines of a shallow porch and the balanced proportions of the entrance and windows on the front and sides. *Warren, Conneticut.*

FOLLOWING PAGE: The Cathedral of St. Francis in Santa Fe, New Mexico, integrates the low simplicity of the Mission buildings of the Francisco friars with solid twin towers, not unlike the massive ones of the feudal Romanesque cathedral. The front façade is decorated with the central rose window of the Gothic cathedral. Its striped arches are reminiscent of the striped marble of Spanish cathedrals influenced by Moorish design. *Santa Fe, New Mexico.*

BELOW: The altar is virtually non-existent in this colonial replica of the interior of St. Martin-in-the-Fields, London. The architect of Christ Church in Philadelphia has slightly "opened up" Gibbs' interior design with a modification to the closed box pews. *Philadelphia, Pennsylvannia.*

found its way to the American colonies soon after it was published in 1727. Christ Church in Cambridge, Massachusetts, was designed by Peter Harrison in 1761, after one of Gibb's plans. Christ Church is made of wood and is far simpler than St. Martin's. It has no upper galleries, and its columns support a simple, coved ceiling. This simplicity in design was not only practical, but also attuned to the Protestant taste for sobriety in church architecture. The style was called Georgian, after the King of England, George III.

King George may have suffered from madness, but the architectural style named after him and modeled on Neoclassical buildings is thought to be the best and most balanced that England has produced. It is self-assured, and exudes a material pride equal to that of a European town for its Gothic cathedral.

James Gibb, whose church of St. Martin-in-the-Fields in London is one of the most imitated.

The basic plan of St. Martin's is that of a galleried, rectangular hall with a portico and steeple. Built at the height of the Baroque in 1722, St. Martin-in-the-Fields was an exercise in interior understatement. It contains the box pews that were usual in England, and upper galleries attached to stately Corinthian columns. The altar is shadowed by the prominence of the raised pulpit. Only the plaster decoration and the curved bays that flank the chancel whisper faint acknowledgment to the architecture of the Italian Baroque of Bernini and his peers.

Gibb's influence was enhanced by the publication of his designs for churches in his *Book of Architecture*, a volume which

LEFT: James Gibb's St. Martin-in-the-Fields was completed in 1726 and became one of the most copied of churches of its period. The central Gothic spire on a classical portico balances reason with spiritual aspiration. *London, England.*

ABOVE: St. Michael's church in Charleston, South Carolina, is modelled on Gibb's St. Martin-in-the-Fields design of a central tower and a classical portico. The architect of St. Michael's has allowed himself more freedom in the design of the spire. *Charleston, South Carolina.*

BELOW: St. Patrick's Cathedral in Manhattan was built between 1858 and 1888 in white marble and stone. Its design is based upon Cologne Cathedral, whose architects strove for extreme height and lightness in design. *New York.*

RIGHT: This massive, white square tower with its Romanesque arches could be mistaken for a Norman cathedral made from English limestone. In fact, it is the Church of Annunciation in Houston, Texas.

The Georgian style was the late incarnation of the late Baroque and Neoclassical churches of Christopher Wren. It is the style that the wealthy congregations of Boston and Newport chose when they were ready for a more formal and elegant church. These early Georgian churches displayed a front tower topped by a spire, a main entrance at one end of an oblong plan, and a longitudinal aisle separating the box pews—simplicity at its most restrained and refined.

The Gothic Revival

The Gothic Revival was the architectural and religious movement of the nineteenth century; the English were the most energetic proponents of the style. Neoclassicism remained popular in America, but it would feel the effect of the Gothic Revival, which carried with it a strong current of religious fervor. The English imported the Gothic Revival to their colonies in

ABOVE: The Gothic Revival that took England by storm in the nineteenth century reached the wealthier congregations in the United States, just as Gibbs' church design had reached the well-to-do congregations of the colonies. This "Edwardian" brick church is in Brooklyn Heights. *Brooklyn, New York.*

ABOVE: The Basilica of Notre Dame was completed in 1829, and is an enormous Neo-Gothic church. The spacious interior was designed by Victor Bourgeau to recreate the atmosphere of a lavish medieval church. Enormous stained-glass windows and a blue vaulted ceiling enhances the effect of medieval "Gothic light." *Montreal, Canada.*

Australia and, of course, to North America, where Gothic and Romanesque cathedrals began to rise in the cities.

American architects had the luxury of building for large, wealthy communities, and they were able to use the form of the medieval church to original ends. Most of these cathedrals were built by Catholics, but the Episcopal Church, which had strong ties to the Anglican Church, also built cathedrals such as St. John the Divine in New York City.

The Cathedral of St. John the Divine is still under construction. A contemporary example of the difficulties of financing the construction of a huge cathedral, it has established a stone-masonry and sculpture workshop to revive the medieval art of decoration.

The Gothic was not the only classic form to be revived. Neo-Romanesque, Neo–Early Christian, and Neo-Byzantine also had their advocates. Many churches in old but newly interpreted styles were constructed during the nineteenth century. The church of St. Vincent de Paul in Paris is Neoclassical, styled after Constantine's basilica and built in the nineteenth century. Trinity Church in Boston, begun in 1872, renewed the Romanesque style, but the lavish interior decoration and its amazing roof are clearly nineteenth-century accomplishments. And London's Westminster Cathedral, begun in 1895, was built in the Byzantine style.

It is impossible to generalize about the diversity of contemporary church architecture, or, for that matter, to know what its future may bring. In his book *The Architecture of Australia*, J. M. Freeland writes:

A country's architecture is a near-perfect record of its history. Every building captures in a physical form the climate and resources of a country's geography; the social, economic, technological, and political conditions of its society; and the moral, philosophical, aesthetic, and spiritual values of its people.

To look back and admire the devotion, invention, and ambition of church builders throughout history is to undertake a lengthy and glorious trip through the architectural and spiritual history of mankind.

GLOSSARY

AISLE—The part of a church that runs parallel to the main areas—nave, choir, and transept—and is separated from them by an arcade.

APSE—The circular, semicircular, or angular end of a church, usually located in the east end.

ARCADE—A series of arches on piers or columns.

BASILICA—A building that consists of a central space between two arcades or colonnades surmounted by a wall with windows, and flanked by lower side aisles.

BOSS—An ornamental projection covering the ribs of a vault.

CAPITAL—The form, often decorated and usually of stone, that supplies the visual transition between the top of a column and whatever the column supports.

CATHEDRAL—A church of any size that contains the cathedra, or bishop's chair.

CHOIR—Traditionally, the section of the church where the choir stands to sing; it is usually east of the transept and is sometimes raised above the level of the nave.

CLERESTORY (or *CLEARSTOREY*)—The wall of the church rising above the roofs of the flanking aisles and containing windows for lighting the central part of the church.

CROWN—The highest part of an arch, where the locking keystone is located.

ICONOSTASIS—A screen decorated with icons that stretches from one wall to the other, and separates the congregation from the sanctuary.

NARTHEX—A porch stretching across the entire width of a church façade.

NAVE—The central area of a church, where the congregation usually sits.

PIER—The pillar or column that supports an arch.

RIB—The stone arch that supports and strengthens a vault.

THRUST—Continuous pressure of one part against another, such as a rafter against a wall.

TRANSEPT—Part of the church at right angles to the nave and choir and, normally, projecting beyond them to give the structure the shape of the cross.

TRIFORIUM—The arcaded story between the nave arcade and the clerestory.

TYMPANUM—The sculptural area enclosed by the arch above the doors of a cathedral.

VAULT—A ceiling or roof made from stone or brick.

BARREL OR TUNNEL VAULT—A continuous arched surface.

FAN VAULT—A vault formed by sections in the form of inverted cones.

GROIN VAULT—A vault formed by the intersection at right angles of two barrel vaults.

LIERNE—A short rib between two other ribs.

PENDANT VAULT—A vault in which the bosses carry downward-pointing projections.

QUADRIPARTITE VAULT—A vault in which the ribs form a simple cross, dividing the bay into four sections.

RIB VAULT—A vault in which the groins, or edges, are outlined by stone ribs.

RIDGE RIB—A rib running longitudinally along the crown of a vault.

SEXPARTITE VAULT—A vault in which there is an extra pair of ribs dividing the bay into six sections.

TEIRCERON—A rib running from the wall to the ridge rib.

LEFT: The construction of Barcelona's Church of the Poor was entrusted to Antonio Gaudí in 1883. Originally conceived as a neo-Gothic cathedral, the entire design was reworked by Gaudí, who made the church the most modern of Gothic structures. The unique front façade is composed of bishop's miters in stone. *Temple de las Sagrada Familia, Barcelona, Spain.*

RIGHT: An enormous gilded statue of the Virgin stands on the belltower of Notre-Dame de la Garde, watching over the port of Marseilles. The church itself is a Neo-Byzantine design completed in the nineteenth century. *Marseilles, France.*

INDEX